Notes

Thank you for purchasing this book.
My hope is this book will encourage
you to read Gods word on a daily basis,
and your see the positvie impact it will
have on your life.

Rhys Horler

Day 1

Rejoice in the Lord always.

I will say it again:

Rejoice!

Philippians 4:4 CSB

Today's Reflection

Day 2

Jesus Christ is the same yesterday
and today and forever!
Hebrews 13:8 NET

Today's Reflection

Day 3

I am able to do all things through him who strengthens me.

Philippians 4:13 CSB

Today's Reflection

Day 4

Now faith is the certainty of
things hoped for,
A proof of things not seen.
Hebrews 11:1 NASB

Today's Reflection

Day 5

Be strong, and let your heart
be courageous,
All you who put your hope in the
Lord.

Psalm 31:24 CSB

Today's Reflection

Day 6

"And now,

Lord,

For what do I wait?

My hope is in You.

Psalm 39:7 NASB

Today's Reflection

Day 7

Rejoice in hope;
Be patient in affliction;
Be persistent in prayer.
Romans 12:12 CSB

Today's Reflection

Day 8

Therefore, since we have been
declared righteous by faith,
We have peace with God through
our Lord Jesus Christ,
Romans 5:1 NET

Today's Reflection

Day 9

As for me,
I will always have hope;
I will praise you more and more.
Psalm 71:14 NIV

Today's Reflection

Day 10

For surely there is a hereafter,
And your hope will not be cut off.
Proverbs 23:18 NKJV

Today's Reflection

Day 11

But I will look to the Lord;
I will wait for the God of
my salvation.
My God will hear me.
                    Micah 7:7 CSB

Today's Reflection

Day 12

Your faith and love have arisen from
the hope laid up for you in heaven,
Which you have heard about in
the message of truth,
The gospel.
Colossians 1:5 NET

Today's Reflection

Day 13

Do everything in love.
1 Corinthians 16:14 NIV

Today's Reflection

Day 14

I desperately long for your deliverance.
I find hope in your word.

Psalm 119:81 NET

Today's Reflection

Day 15

For God so loved the world that He gave His only begotten Son, That whoever believes in Him should not perish but have everlasting life.

John 3:16 NJKV

Today's Reflection

Day 16

My command is this:
Love each other as I have loved you.

John 15:12 NIV

Today's Reflection

Day 17

But God demonstrates his
own love toward us,
In that while we were still sinners,
Christ died for us.
Romans 5:8 NASB

Today's Reflection

Day 18

Speak up,
Judge righteously,
And defend the cause of the
oppressed and needy.

Proverbs 31:9 CSB

Today's Reflection

Day 19

And we know that all things work
together for good for those who love God,
Who are called according to
his purpose,
Romans 8:28 NET

Today's Reflection

Day 20

For if you forgive other people
when they sin against you,
Your heavenly Father
will also forgive you.
Matthew 6:14 NIV

Today's Reflection

Day 21

Come to Me,

All you who labor and are heavy laden,

And I will give you rest.

Matthew 11:28 NKJV

Today's Reflection

Day 22

And over all these virtues put on love,

Which binds them all together

in perfect unity.

Colossians 3:14 NIV

Today's Reflection

Day 23

In peace I will lie down and sleep,

For you alone,

Lord,

Make me dwell in safety.

Psalm 4:8 NIV

Today's Reflection

Day 24

But You,
O Lord,
Are a shield for me,
My glory and the One who
lifts up my head.
Psalm 3:3 NKJV

Today's Reflection

Day 25

The Lord is for me;
I will not fear;
What can man do to me?

Psalm 118:6 NKJV

Today's Reflection

Day 26

For God did not give us a Spirit
of fear but of power and love
and self-control.

2 Timothy 1:7 NET

Today's Reflection

Day 27

Learn to do good;

Seek justice,

Rebuke the oppressor;

Defend the fatherless,

Plead for the widow.

Isaiah 1:17 NKJV

Today's Reflection

Day 28

But Jesus looked at them and said,
"With men it is impossible,
But not with God;
For with God all things are possible."
Mark 10:27 NKJV

Today's Reflection

Day 29

Let's not become discouraged
in doing good,
For in due time we will reap,
If we do not become weary.
Galatians 6:9 NASB

Today's Reflection

Day 30

For I am sure of this very thing,
That the one who began a good work
in you will perfect it until the day of
Christ Jesus.
Philippians 1:6 NET

Today's Reflection

Day 31

The Lord will fight for you,
And you can be still."
Exodus 14:14 NET

Today's Reflection

Day 32

That no one should be shaken by
these afflictions;
For you yourselves know that we
are appointed to this.
1 Thessalonians 3:3 NKJV

Today's Reflection

Day 33

We love because He first loved us.

1 John 4:19 NIV

Today's Reflection

Day 34

He says,

"Be still, and know that I am God;

I will be exalted among the nations,

I will be exalted in the earth."

Psalm 46:10 NIV

Today's Reflection

Day 35

Bears all things,
Believes all things,
Hopes all things,
Endures all things.
1 Corinthians 13:7 NKJV

Today's Reflection

Day 36

So that we who had already put our
hope in Christ might bring praise
to his glory.

Ephesians 1:12 CSB

Today's Reflection

Day 37

But I hope,

In the Lord Jesus,

To send Timothy to you shortly,

So that I also may be encouraged

when I learn of your condition.

Philippians 2:19 NASB

Today's Reflection

Day 38

Even when I must walk through
the darkest valley,
I fear no danger,
For you are with me;
Your rod and your staff reassure me
Psalm 23:4 NET

Today's Reflection

Day 39

To them God has chosen to make
known among the Gentiles the
glorious riches of this mystery,
Which is Christ in you,
The hope of glory.
Colossians 1:27 NIV

Today's Reflection

Day 40

Hatred stirs up strife,
But love covers all sins.
Proverbs 10:12 NKJV

Today's Reflection

Day 41

Wives,

Submit to your husbands,

As is fitting in the Lord.

Husbands,

Love your wives and do not

be embittered against them.

Colossians 3:18-19 NET

Today's Reflection

Day 42

Set me like a cylinder seal over
your heart,
Like a signet on your arm
For love is as strong as death,
Passion is as unrelenting as Sheol.
Its flames burst forth,
It is a blazing flame.
Song of Solomon 8:6 NET

Today's Reflection

Day 43

Fixing our eyes on Jesus,
the pioneer and perfecter of faith.
For the joy set before him he
endured the cross,
Scorning its shame,
And sat down at the right hand of
the throne of God.
Hebrews 12:2 NIV

Today's Reflection

Day 44

A friend loves at all times,
And a brother is born for adversity.
Proverbs 17:17 NKJV

Today's Reflection

Day 45

The Lord is my shepherd;
I have what I need.

Psalm 23:1 CSB

Today's Reflection

Day 46

For the righteousness of God
is revealed in the gospel from
faith to faith,
Just as it is written,
"The righteous by faith will live."
Romans 1:17 NET

Today's Reflection

Day 47

Once you were not a people,
But now you are the people of God;
Once you had not received mercy,
But now you have received mercy.

1 Peter 2:10 NIV

Today's Reflection

Day 48

Beloved,

Now we are children of God;

And it has not yet been revealed

what we shall be,

But we know that when He

is revealed,

We shall be like Him,

For we shall see Him as He is.

1 John 3:2 NKJV

Today's Reflection

Day 49

And that Christ may dwell in
your hearts through faith.
I pray that you,
Being rooted and firmly
established in love.
Ephesians 3:17 CSB

Today's Reflection

Day 50

But let justice flow like water,

And righteousness,

Like an unfailing stream.

Amos 5:24 CSB

Today's Reflection

Day 51

Be on your guard;

Stand firm in the faith;

Be courageous;

Be strong.

1 Corinthians 16:13 NIV

Today's Reflection

Day 52

Through the Lord's mercies we are
not consumed,
Because His compassions fail not.
Lamentations 3:22 NKJV

Today's Reflection

Day 53

What,

Then,

Are we to say about these things?
If God is for us,
Who is against us?

Romans 8:31 CSB

Today's Reflection

Day 54

God is our refuge and strength,
A very ready help in trouble.

Psalm 46:1 NASB

Today's Reflection

Day 55

Taste and see that the Lord is good.
How blessed is the one who takes
shelter in him.

Psalm 34:8 NET

Today's Reflection

Day 56

Give thanks to the Lord,

For he is good;

His love endures forever.

Psalm 107:1 NIV

Today's Reflection

Day 57

The name of the Lord is a strong tower;

The righteous run to it and are safe.

Proverbs 18:10 NKJV

Today's Reflection

Day 58

Haven't I commanded you:
Be strong and courageous?
Do not be afraid or discouraged,
For the Lord your God is with
you wherever you go."

Joshua 1:9 CSB

Today's Reflection

Day 59

These things I have spoken to you so
that in Me you may have peace.
In the world you have tribulation,
But take courage;
I have overcome the world."
John 16:33 NASB

Today's Reflection

Day 60

When you pass through the waters,
I am with you;
When you pass through the streams,
They will not overwhelm you.
When you walk through the fire,
You will not be burned;
The flames will not harm you.

Isaiah 43:2 NET

Today's Reflection

Day 61

Surely God is my salvation;
I will trust and not be afraid.
The Lord,
The Lord himself,
Is my strength and my defense;
He has become my salvation."

Isaiah 12:2 NIV

Today's Reflection

Day 62

But those who wait on the Lord
Shall renew their strength;
They shall mount up with
wings like eagles,
They shall run and not be weary,
They shall walk and not faint.
Isaiah 40:31 NKJV

Today's Reflection

Day 63

Love must be sincere.

Hate what is evil;

Cling to what is good.

Romans 12:9 NIV

Today's Reflection

Day 64

My blessing is on those people who trust in me,

Jeremiah 17:7 NET

Today's Reflection

Day 65

""The Lord bless you
and keep you;
The Lord make his face shine on you
and be gracious to you;
The Lord turn his face toward you
and give you peace."'
Numbers 6:24-26 NIV

Today's Reflection

Day 66

Therefore I say to you,
Whatever things you ask
when you pray,
Believe that you receive them,
And you will have them.
Mark 11:24 NKJV

Today's Reflection

Day 67

Rejoice always,
Pray constantly,
Give thanks in everything;
For this is God's will for you in
Christ Jesus.
1 Thessalonians 5:16-18 CSB

Today's Reflection

Day 68

Commit your works to the Lord,
And your plans will be established.

Proverbs 16:3 NASB

Today's Reflection

Day 69

So do not fear,

For I am with you;

Do not be dismayed,

For I am your God.

I will strengthen you and help you;

I will uphold you with my righteous

right hand.

Isaiah 41:10 NIV

Today's Reflection

Day 70

May I hear about your loyal
love in the morning,
For I trust in you.
Show me the way I should go,
Because I long for you.
Psalm 143:8 NET

Today's Reflection

Day 71

For I know what I have planned
for you,
' Says the Lord.
' I have plans to prosper you,
Not to harm you.
I have plans to give you a future
filled with hope.
Jeremiah 29:11 NET

Today's Reflection

Day 72

For we walk by faith,
Not by sight.

2 Corinthians 5:7 CSB

Today's Reflection

Day 73

You must serve the Lord your God,
And he will bless your bread and
your water,
And I will remove sickness from
your midst.
Exodus 23:25 NET

Today's Reflection

Day 74

With all humility and gentleness,

With patience,

Putting up with one another in love,

Ephesians 4:2 NET

Today's Reflection

Day 75

Why are you cast down,
O my soul?
And why are you disquieted
within me?
Hope in God;
For I shall yet praise Him,
The help of my countenance
and my God.
Psalm 42:11 NKJV

Today's Reflection

Day 76

If I give all I possess to the poor

and give over my body to hardship

that I may boast,

But do not have love,

I gain nothing.

1 Corinthians 13:13 NIV

Today's Reflection

Day 77

And not only that,

But we also boast in our afflictions,

Because we know that affliction

produces endurance,

Endurance produces proven character,

And proven character produces hope.

Romans 5:3-4 CSB

Today's Reflection

Day 78

You are my hiding place and
my shield;
I wait for Your word.
Psalm 119:114 NASB

Today's Reflection

Day 79

But if we hope for what we do not see,
We eagerly wait for it with endurance.

Romans 8:25 NET

Today's Reflection

Day 80

Hope deferred makes the heart sick,
But a longing fulfilled is like a tree
of life.
Proverbs 13:12 NET

Today's Reflection

Day 81

"The Lord is my portion,"
Says my soul,
"Therefore I hope in Him!"
Lamentations 3:24 NKJV

Today's Reflection

Day 82

Guide me in your truth and teach me,
For you are the God of my salvation;
I wait for you all day long.
Psalm 25:5 CSB

Today's Reflection

Day 83

Let Your favor,

Lord,

Be upon us,

Just as we have waited for you.

Psalm 33:22 NASB

Today's Reflection

Day 84

I rely on the Lord.

I rely on him with my whole being;

I wait for his assuring word.

Psalm 130:5 NET

Today's Reflection

Day 85

Now hope does not disappoint,
Because the love of God has been
poured out in our hearts by the
Holy Spirit who was given to us.
Romans 5:5 NKJV

Today's Reflection

Day 86

But in your hearts regard
Christ the Lord as holy,
Ready at any time to give a defense
to anyone who asks you for a reason
for the hope that is in you.
1 Peter 3:15 CSB

Today's Reflection

Day 87

When I am afraid,
I will put my trust in You.
Psalm 56:3 NASB

Today's Reflection

Day 88

There is one body and one Spirit,
Just as you too were called to the
one hope of your calling,
Ephesians 4:4 NET

Today's Reflection

Day 89

I pray that the eyes of your heart may be
enlightened in order that you may know
the hope to which he has called you,
The riches of his glorious inheritance
in his holy people,
Ephesians 1:18 NIV

Today's Reflection

Day 90

So shall the knowledge of wisdom be
to your soul;
If you have found it,
There is a prospect,
And your hope will not be cut off.
Proverbs 24:14 NKJV

Today's Reflection

Day 91

The hope of the righteous is joy,
But the expectation of the
wicked perishes.
Proverbs 10:28 NET

Today's Reflection

Day 92

God "will repay each person according to what they have done."

Romans 2:6 NIV

Today's Reflection

Day 93

"Blessed are those who hunger
and thirst for righteousness,
For they will be satisfied.
Matthew 5:6 NET

Today's Reflection

Day 94

Treasures gained by wickedness do not profit,

But righteousness delivers from death.

Proverbs 10:2 NET

Today's Reflection

Day 95

For He made Him who knew
no sin to be sin for us,
That we might become the
righteousness of God in Him.
2 Corinthians 5:21 NKJV

Today's Reflection

Day 96

The eyes of the Lord are on
the righteous,
And his ears are open to their
cry for help.
Psalm 34:15 CSB

Today's Reflection

Day 97

For the grace of God has appeared,

Bringing salvation to all people,

Instructing us to deny ungodliness and

worldly desires and to live sensibly,

Righteously,

And in a godly manner in the

present age,

Titus 2:11-12 NASB

Today's Reflection

Day 98

Peacemakers who sow in peace reap
a harvest of righteousness.

James 3:18 NIV

Today's Reflection

Day 99

A wicked person earns deceptive wages,

But one who sows righteousness gets

a true reward.

Proverbs 11:18 NASB

Today's Reflection

Day 100

Therefore,
Confess your sins to one another
and pray for one another,
So that you may be healed.
The prayer of a righteous person
is very powerful in its effect.
James 5:16 CSB

Today's Reflection

Notes

Notes

Printed in Great Britain
by Amazon